THE DESIRE LINE

THE DESIRE LINE

Memory & Impermanence

Poems and Photographs by

Sven Davisson

Rebel Satori Press

New Orleans

Published in the United States of America by
REBEL SATORI PRESS
www.rebelsatoripress.com

Copyright © 2017 by Sven Davisson. All rights reserved. Except for brief passages quoted in newspaper, magazine, radio, television, or online reviews, no part of this book may be reproduced in any form or any means, electronic or mechanical, including photocopying, recording, or information or retrieval system, without the permission in writing from the publisher. Please do not participate in or encourage piracy of copyrighted materials in violation of the author's rights. Purchase only authorized editions.

Library of Congress Cataloging-in-Publication Data

Names: Davisson, Sven, author.
Title: The desire line : memory & impermanence / Sven Davisson.
Description: New Orleans : Rebel Satori Press, 2017.
Identifiers: LCCN 2016027636 | ISBN 9781608641048 (pbk.)
Classification: LCC PS3604.A978256 A6 2017 | DDC 811/.6--dc23
LC record available at https://lccn.loc.gov/2016027636

*To Nate, Ricky, Jackson, Lafitte,
and the memory of Rex*

Table of Contents

Musings: by way of an introduction   i

The Desire Line   1

Memory

Mandalay	9
Wabi-sabi	13
Remind Me	14
The Abigail, 1628	18
Horizons	23
Eight-Dollar George	31
End of the World in New York City	34
Muse	37
La Track	40
I Always Thought Andy Would Be There	42
"Recalling my father's midnight snack…"	45
You Live	46
"Some moments…"	51
Memory	52
Jason Cycle	55

Impermanence

Metta	75
"the train whistle…"	79
Dinosaurs in denouement	81
Equally Buddha	82
Friendship	85
"A clipping…"	86
NOLA Zazen	89

"A bucket…"	93
3am Tweeker	95
Root Guru	96
Silver Halide Crystals	99
Sewing the Rakusu	103
The Impermanence of Never	104
The Space Between	106
About the Photographs	108
Acknowledgements	110
About the Author	114

Musings: by way of an introduction

Noted photographer Sally Mann has often commented on her observation that photography destroys memory. In conversation with Charlie Rose at the 92nd Str Y, Mann reflected on the photographic image's tendency toward "subverting," "displacing," "undercutting," and "stealing from memory." All too quickly, reminiscence of the photograph supplants memory of the originating event.

Perhaps it is the ubiquitous proliferation of the image over the past century and a half, that has posed a greater and more observable threat. Increasing since the invention of chemically recording light as static image, the petrified depictions of fractions of seconds are now everywhere. The photographic image solidifies a moment or an approximation thereof. Accurate or misleading, that moment is then mythologized as truth. The image, reified, open to industrial replication and endless reproduction, occludes memory.

Memory itself is mutable enough on its own, and this may be precisely the intersection where memory and photography find their mutual transfection. In her book *The Twenty-four Hour Mind*, Rosalind Cartwright argues that "memory is never a precise duplicate of the original; instead, it is a continuing act of creation." I would add 're-creation.' Memory becomes saga. Saga becomes legend. Legend becomes myth. The gilt Icon eventually replaces the saint it represents.

In the almost 200 years since Nicéphore Niépce made the first light-fast camera photo (1824) and Henry Fox Talbot produced the first silver chloride negative (1835), the photographic image (analog then digital) has been on a head-spinning ascendency. We now live in an unprecedented world of images. The gilt icon of ages past, the altar triptych with its eternal dramatis personae, was a singular awe-inducing experience. Modernity—as encapsulated in the endless reproducibility of images and words—has given rise to a new magical landscape, personal and pagan in its fetishism.

Susan Sontag writes in *On Photography*, "All photographs are *memento mori*." They evidence the subject's mutability and mortality, she observes. They capture an instance in time that will never occur again. Living or dead, the faces that look back at us from family snapshots are no more. Time has moved on, that fractional moment is past. Every photograph is an evidentiary exhibit of impermanence, itself impermanent as light slowly fades that which light and chemistry created.

In truth a photograph is only the approximation of the single moment. Even this is a treachery. In fact a photograph captures some fraction of a second. The image and technology approaches the single moment in halflife steps but will never attain the dimensionless point.

In the *Heart Sutra* Avalokiteśvara tells Śariputra, "Form is emptiness. Emptiness is form." Of photography

Sontag tells us, "Surrealism lies at the heart of the photographic enterprise: in the very creation of a duplicate world, of a reality in the second degree, narrower but more dramatic than the one perceived by natural vision." What color is the mind? What are we taking a picture of when we depress the shutter? Is it capturing the scene in front of the lens, or the mental vision behind my eyes? Photographic truth or my idiosyncratic mental editing of what is seen?

The world we inhabit is an edited montage of stimuli. William Burroughs described it as a "cut-up". We make choices. Sontag described the act of photography as inherently violent. Meanwhile, Chogyam Trungpa Rinpoche extolls us to be nonaggressive in our art. How does one reconcile these seemingly incompatible positions? When we frame our vision, constraining the infinite into the finite dimensions of the ground glass, what mind is behind the vision?

Reportage is seen as embodying photographic truth, but it is often an aggressive act toward the subject, the viewer, or both. The war photographer has brought incredibly important evidence of atrocities. It's hard to cover up when a picture speaks a thousand words. How is the photographer exempted from the damnation of the observer who did not act?

How does one frame a still image with no mind? Or maybe more appropriately, how do we make an image *of* no mind. Trungpa describes this as realization of 'unconditional symbolism,' where we appreciate "the empty gap of our state of mind" and begin "to project ourselves into that non-reference point."

Is a photograph the past, the now, or something yet to be? What are these catalogs of images and words? reference points in a personal cosmology? a rotating exhibition of impermanence in a mental museum?

In my own ancestral mythology, there is in the land of Asgard, home of the gods, Yggdrasil, the World Tree. At its roots, is the well of Urd around which gather the three sisters, the norns. Urd is the past. Skuld is that which is to come. Between them the present, Verdandi. Most telling, her name translates to "becoming". The present moment is not stasis but potency.

New Orleans, 2017

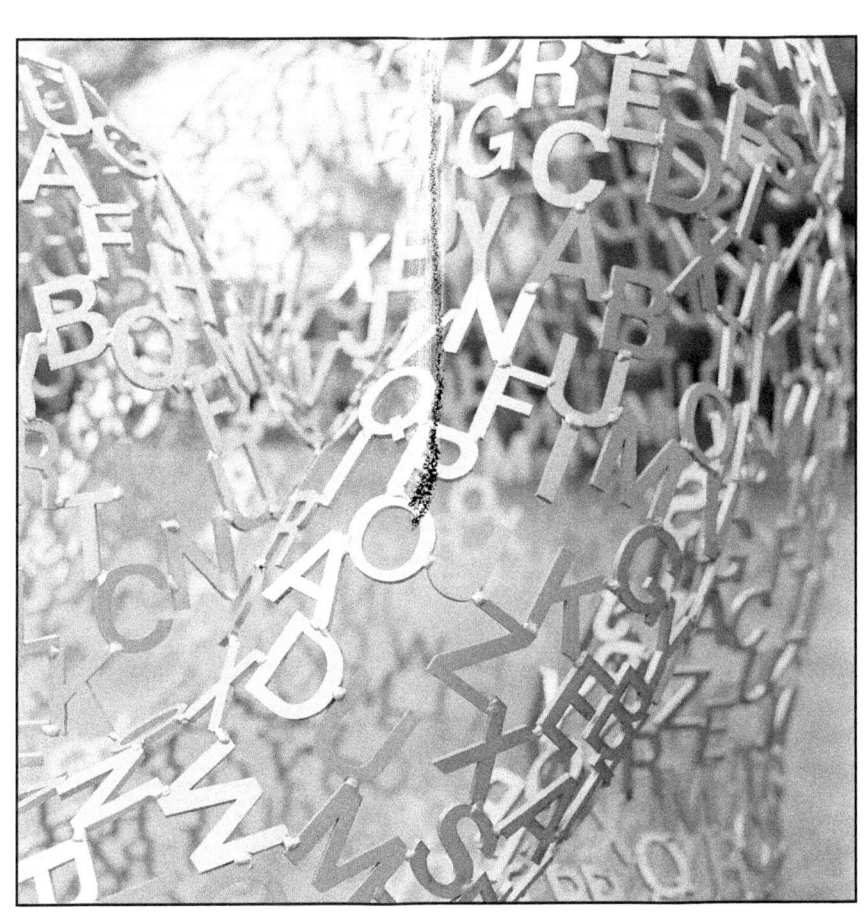

The Desire Line

The air is crisp on a December morning
a truck just outside the window
pours concrete filling in holes
where gas lines were recently replaced
patching an infrastructure
as glorious in decay as this city
where the lines of desire,
death, and disintegration
intersect with such
heart-stopping poetry.

Papa Legba is at the door—
St. Peter at the gate;
Baron Samedi looks on impassively
seeing into two worlds,
absinthe and unmarked graves;
and Our Lady of the Three Marks
sitting in her silence
one hand on her lap the other
holding a pipe to her lips.

The Desire Line,
parallel veins of blood
salty and ferrous

connecting back through
ancestors and bonds
stronger than genetics,
cables of semen arcing
their current through the air
keeping this whole show
on the tracks.

Ambushing ghost memories
powerful enough to permanently
etch themselves into consciousness
a temporal existence
now retained in stylized
partially idealized recollection

I meditate with ancestors as petite gods
I sit vigil with their existence—
one that is as present now
as the last time we met,
spoke on the phone,
or touched in intimacy.
Present now but different,
blunted, worn soft at the corners
like the remnants of the history
in this city that push
through to the present
and so frequently lift its residents
out of the everyday

like disused streetcar rails
and cobblestones
break through cracking asphalt.

A catalog of artifacts:
my father's pocket knife;
the smoky smell of
my grandmother's scotch;
the naked santa from George's mantel
from Oct 1 through 12th Night
hairy chested and priapic;
a rectamgle of agate
polished to reveal the devil
with flames at his back
and a monkey's face;
plastic St. Patrick Day beads
with its lucky clover—
shiny and metallic;
the gentle testing hand
of a handsome stranger
in the charged darkness.

The handwritten dedication
at the front of your last book;
a siouixsie & the banshees song
randomly playing in the background;
a red velvet dress and blond wig
when we helped clean

out your apartment
that last time;
and the memory so strong
that it lingers despite the loss
of any physical mementos—
lost to the breakers of time,
to frequent moves of youth,
and the endless petty dramas
that eclipsed the long story arc
but could not dim the light
radiating from a smile
in the few pictures
that survive.

Shelves of textual ancestors
form the backdrop of my shrine
Burroughs, Ginsberg, Gysin,
Acker, Karouac, Wojnarowicz
Dreams, Cats, and Alcohol.
Straight Heart's Delight brought me
into the real world.
"Kraj Mahales" gave me
the red string of second birth—
Dharma Bums my original jukai;
The Wild Boys and *Port of Saints*
my shamanic initiation
between the worlds.

The lands of Plague. the bardo, and
the dangerous road to immortality.
Whiskey soaked reality visions,
new myths, scars, and magics.
Chanting your words as mantras.

La Madama, fortuna,
the Nine of Cups,
a blue candle to open the road
the color where memory
and prosperity intersect
on the octarine spectrum.

The blanketing sound of rain,
the steady drip from the eaves
onto the air conditioner,
the glow of candles
smells of pomegranate and cassis,
Eau de parfum Reve d'Or.
Snifter of water and
a touch of bourbon.

Memory

Mandalay

You can never return to Mandalay.
Even in a dream, the gate remains barred.
No supernatural power exists that is capable
of taking you back to your own past.
Nature always comes into her own.
Time overgrows memory with delusion.
Falsehoods triumph in the end.
Recollection becomes crowded,
dark and uncontrolled—phantoms lurking
at the edges mysterious in the English mist.
Painful moments remain white and naked;
while pleasures become attenuated,
less tangible the tighter one attempts to hold onto them
delicate cultivars overgrown by the fecundity of pain.

Returning home, to the place where one grew up,
becomes a strange embrace.
Things have changed. The course of time
has eroded deeper into the bedrock,
while the fingers of nature encroach
with no one to cut them back.
Here and there you recognize landmarks.

In the midst of it all, like a locked jewel box

cradled by its environment—
simultaneously foreign and familiar—rests memory.
It skulks behind the underbrush
a crumbled rampart set against your return.

No matter how hard you try to recapture
the good times buried in those memories,
Mrs. Danvers is always there standing
a dark specter at the window.
You can see her just there in a movement of the curtains
among the wreckage of what you thought was.
The things you would have preferred to forget—
the isolation, the childish cruelties—
are there lurking as furtive unrest
and a general sense of trepidation.

Wabi-sabi

We move through the world from emptiness.
Our now is non-existent compared
to the time witnessed by earth and rock.
Mountains rise and rivers carve new valleys.
Ephemeral evidence marks our passing—
bent leaves of grass after we walk on,
the wet sole print of a sneaker
fading on rough split logs.

The relationships you fell in love with
watching Queer As Folk before coming out…
"Let's Get Soaking Wet" and
"It's Raining Men" anthems cutting through
inflection points of passion and sadness…

Beauty overtakes what is left behind—
the stone foundation overgrown
ferns splitting mortar from fieldstone
an ex's new boyfriend poses
where once there was window glass.
The graffiti artist coopts a crack
for his own purposes
a curve becomes a beret
for a monoacled artist.

Remind Me

Visiting Allen Ginsberg's Beat snapshots
at the National Gallery of Art
an unanticipated sadness
black crows circle out of mind
grainy blackandwhite ghosts
of my own childhood
the skeleton of time
reminds me
hours spent discussing
Shelley's 'Ode to the Westwind'
as breath machine
Ozymandias and impermanence
Remind me
when
we meet again
and now years later
here we are
fading snapshots
behind glass
the mundane and casual
archived and labeled
national memory
occluding personal ones
Remind me

how handsome Peter was
dead now just three months
as I move through the galleries
images set out in chronological order
I note how many lives are end dated
take note of the rare few that are not
reflecting on life impermanent
as the
chemicals
that form the emulsions
fading minutely before me
Remind me
the second day of Ango
an image of Gary Snyder
catches my eye
and makes me smile
young thin unexpectedly handsome
Unsui's koromo with rakusu
standing in his garden
Kyoto, July 1963
Remind me
the grey in your beard
as you lit a cigarette
beneath a NO SMOKING sign
answering a student question
quoting Trungpa
on enlightenment
stepping on the step that isn't there

my own mental snapshots
turning to gray
and beginning to fade
Remind me
your words
written on the back
of a postcard
an aerial view of Nashville
postmark new york
the same hand beneath
each of these images
the next morning
sitting in meditation
thoughts fighting back
pulling me toward poetry
rebelling with a cascade of words
that have not come in months
your scribbled words…
Remind me
when next we meet
whether it be in Maine
at Naropa
or somewhere on the moon

The Abigail, 1628

Among the earliest immigrants
on my mother's side
were Charles Gott
and Gift Palmer
who arrived in Salem
with John Endecott
first governor of the
Massachusetts Bay Colony
the summer of 1628
departing Weymouth
on the *Abigail*
disembarking in the
new world on Sept 9

For my father's part
his forbear William
arrived from Scotland in 1685
an indentured servant
and later married Magaret
the daughter of covenanters
who accompanied their
banished son William
aboard the *Henry and Francis*

Tracing back family lore
along the geometric
recession of ancestors
to Mayflower notables
and the dead ends
of lost records
generations before
current memory
the fading ghosts
of stories becoming
transparent with
each successive passing
the muted colors
of ancient tartan
dyes lightening
with each day

My great aunt often
claimed to be a witch
Everyone knew that women
born on the offshore islands
were, she claimed
Inching back through
the meiotic cleaving
I cross paths with
Goody Foster, née Alcock,
who died 1692
awaiting execution

in the Salem jail
and the midwife
Grace Pratt accused
of witchcraft 1653

There's blood and fire
and pandemic
the Battle of Flodden Field
death alongside James IV
of Jacobite sympathies
a treasured heirloom
carried with them
to the New World
the French and Indian Wars
colonists fighting
in the Revolution
and the Tory branch
of the family fleeing
to the British Maritimes
the hardship of first winters
sickness and deprivation

My bóveda, a shrine
of photographs and artifacts:
a bone handled pocket knife,
a shaving mug, green rock,
collar de Yamaya,
beach rocks and sea glass,

fading swatch of tartan,
and crest badge
Sapienter si sincere
Wisely if sincerely

Horizons

for Ruth Moore

the sisters in my grandmother s family
all had nicknames weezie, tug, and up
uppy to the generations of children
who played at her feet
with the small zoo of oversized crocheted
animals hidden in the hall closet

summer sunday afternoons
as the garden progressed to harvest
sitting in the living room
when her bad foot prevented
her from making the trek
across the lighthouse road
an ashtray impossibly full
of cigarette butts to her left
a tall glass of light brown liquid
ginger ale or scotch and water
depending on whether the sun
had descended below
the window s meeting rail

trading books and authors
allen ginsberg on my part
archie and mehetible on hers

she wrote a poem at the time
offering a young poet
the advice of a comma well placed
a wonderful irony while
recommending the work
of a cockroach who couldn t capitalize
the shift plus letter keys
being too long a reach

stories swirled the room
fanciful and mysterious
and with a spry mischievousness
that belied her 80-some years
skipper mcbride and
his lucky ammonite,
the unlucky randell,
ringgold the pirate,
poor old sam who once
mistook a whale for a u-boat,
and the haunting creatures
of the maine woods:
the ravenous wendigo,
will-am-alones rolling
their poison balls
sowing nightmares
while you sleep,
harry-toothed dr. pillgarlic,
and the hang-downs

tales of the ancestral home
a mile from the harbor s mouth
an island with its indian middens,
fairy houses, pioneer communalism
of island privilege, and the unmarked
graves of black island quarrymen
who washed ashore in a time
precedent to current memory

a small house full of treasures
collected and catalogued
a pinched bottle
that belches when poured,
a wabanaki arrowhead,
a small milky-green block of beryl,
an agate tumbled smooth
to reveal the devil in hell,
drawers full of negatives and slides
travel photography to fine art
sorted sleeved and labeled

walls lined with books
field guides to everything
that one might find
in the natural world
from mushrooms, to feathers,
to wildflowers, to spiders
reminders of friends

a cat teased from stone
by the sculptor s hand
of chenoweth hall
a note from e.b. white
bookmarking his
collection of letters

the orchard of heirloom cultivars
curated and grafted for eating,
cooking, and winter storage
the spring at the foot of the field
a clear cool witch s cauldron
encircled in oaken roots
and beached in moss
the english garden its bricks
overgrown with sod
peonies, columbine, and ladies mantle
fighting their way through
the encroaching blackberries
the pink granite marker
edges softened by waves

the outbuildings
homespun museums
to two lives well lived
and a mutual love for art,
craft, literature, the natural world
stones, fossils, and

two-thousand year old tools
the yellow jeep cj
in which i first learned
to drive a standard
its alignment off to the left
after hitting a tree on
a late-night scotch-fueled
drive down to camp

the pilgrams path winding
contemplatively to the shore
stepping over blowdowns
and ducking under widowmakers
old tall spruces
falling like dominos
after the first one
succumbs to a winter nor easter

on the writing desk
hand built with utilitarian beauty
seafoam green horizon 3000
a single line on the paper
rolled onto its roller

i have seen horizons

Eight-Dollar George

Hawaiian shirts and flip flops
red velvet and ostrich plumes
months planning your outfit
for red dress run
pouring over catalogs
at your corner of the bar
the beauty of your creations
floral arrangements
symphonies of color
pollen and fragrance
to that single white gardenia
in a plastic cup that
Dan brought to you each day
All the happy hours spent
sitting on your front steps
"the czar of the stoop"
before the previous owners
put in the metal railings
and spoiled your fun

I've heard the stories.
Everyone has heard the stories!
The trick who only wanted
bus fare home

and a ten was too much
as only he needed eight so
you had to cross the street
and make change at the bar
The cruises, the friendships
the ex-lover youcradled in life
and washed in death
when no one else would
even your own friends
too afraid to come to the house

the smile,
the almost silent cutting quip
your greeting
"There are my babies!"
The endless stream
of your future ex-husbands

"Say 'Goodnight, George'"
Goodnight, George

End of the World in New York City

Someone predicted the Rapture
would be the following Saturday
Judgment Day May 21, 2011
the bible guarantees it
but is unclear on the details
blinding meteor showers?
killer human-eating plants
as in *Day of the Triffids*?
the nuclear holocaust of
Daybreak 2250AD
or *On the Beach*?
fire or ice or indifference?

We take the L train to Manhattan
walk through Central Park
spring's warming sun
bringing people out
to the green grass
exit at E 102nd
and walk up 5th avenue
past the Museum of
the City of New York

then head down to the Village

grab a drink along the way
making our slow progress
toward Ginsberg's last apartment
on East Thirteenth for the
Adaptation Project fund-raiser
run into Bob Holman
on his way out and our way in
he'll be back momentarily
he reassures us
Waiting for others to arrive
Bob Rosenthal gives the readers
an impromptu tutorial on Yiddish
Left to myself I walk
around the rooms
emptied of all their thingnesses
I wonder if there is still
fish chowder in the freezer
Allen's bedroom turned
green room for the night
hardwood floors echoing each step
sound softening as more people arrive
replaced with the gray noise
of a dozen conversations

After the event we head
over to Splash
we drink dance drink
admire a go-go boy

with that just-so-grin
12:01AM Britney Spears'
dance until the world ends
the DJ mixes that perfect moment
of music and irony

the next morning we ride the L train
from Brooklyn into the City again
and grab brunch in Chelsea
then through a street fair
looking for that perfect hat
past the old Limelight, the Sanctuary,
now posh boutiques

Speak Up! reading
at El Museo del Bario
Tato Laviera reading from memory
with such force and presence
Then off to meet
Brandon @ the Boiler-room
on to the Cock Bar post-midnight
finding a place by
the far end of the bar
to admire the boy atop
neon green camo briefs
biohazard inked on his left pec
He kneels down on one knee, smiles,
and earns a few bucks from each of us

Muse

Dark fusion of Erato and Ganymede,
a fire-sorcerer summoning chthonic forces
from places not known by men,
Kaotic emotion splits great fissures
on its way to the surface.
Rock transforms to orange lava
in the Master's forge.
I long to join him in sacrifice
to crash against that sea
to thunder and hiss in steam,
then lie black and spent
once again immovable rock.

Inspiration catches the senses
as distinctive as the scent of diesel—
petro-lust of decaying flesh
echoing strength across millennia.
The fuel to the engine of creativity
sets spark combusting the soul.
Strong, young, favored prince,
volcanic blacksmith at Hel's forge,
his cup is a fiery crucible
in which self melts
to its constituent parts.

Heat separates the ego
from the emptiness.
There is no god
in the silent space
between mortals and eternity.

Sweet flag moves above the water,
Kalamos' sorrowful lament.
The water reed sees its reflection
a reversed twin rippling
in answer to whisper.
I hunger for that inspiration
born in the furnace of another.
The soft counterbalance of flesh
I rest my head on the chest of the Muse
cradled in strong arms like a lyre.

La Track

Beneath Rue St. Catherine
a tall stranger across the dance floor
silhouetted in the dark club
features carved in red blue green lasers
a handsome that makes you lose the beat
or lose yourself to it
this exact now is perfect
this is precisely where in the Universe
I am meant to be
strobes reflect off
small oval glasses just
the right hint of bookish
I make my way across the floor
until I'm standing just close enough
without being obvious
Ricky Martin's "Livin' La Vida Loca"
starts to energize the room
shift pivot till we are
almost dancing together
Cher's "Believe"
I bum a cigarette
even though I don't smoke
he answers with a smile and a light
I lean closer feeling our sweat

rising like steam between us
closer and our lips touch
brief and hot and furtive
he speaks Spanish
and I only English
in a club full of French speakers
I finally find someone
who (hopefully) knows
enough of all three
at that breakthrough
where communication happens
and understanding widens
his eyes light with enthusiasm
as night moves in flesh to morning
there is no more need for words
the silent language of waking
in each others' arms

I Always Thought Andy Would Be There

I Always Thought Andy Would Be There
title of an immature first novel
finished but never published.
Education through teen years
fueled by Vanity Fair, Interview,
Spin and Gordon Merrick novels
Perfect Freedom seeding
an unquenchable devouring
of *Dancer from the Dance,*
Boys on the Rock,
A Boys Own Story,
The Great Urge Downward,
Buccaneer, and *Cody.*
Followed by a river of paperbacks
gleaned from the photocopied
pages of the Wilde Bookshop,
giving way to Allen Ginsberg's
heavenly adonises and
Burroughs' wild boys.

Slick magazine pages
with the salacious and glorious
a glittering mirror of Reagan-era
American excess

Truman Capote slips away
beside Joanne Carson's pool
filled with booze and pills
a last scathingly biting observation
left unspoken on his lips.
That surreal moment on Merv Griffin
when he recounts how Sunny von Bülow
taught him to shoot up

Through the glossy windows
of magazine pages I glimpsed
a confluence of music and art
Soft Cell Frankie Bronski Beat
Mapplethorpe Haring Morrissoe
Hugh Steers, Peter Hujar, and Herb Ritts
David Seidner
One great glittering party
accented by funerals
but like the laughing monk
the corpses held hidden fireworks
I thought the party would last forever

And

I always thought Andy would be there
the barometric constant
of my coming of age

"Recalling my father's midnight snack…"

Recalling my father's midnight snack
vanilla ice cream and codeine
his copy of Blythe's *Games Zen Masters Play*
sitting on the shelf near me now
its cover still stained
with gray smudged clouds
of newsprint from his *Wall Street Journal.*

You Live

Watching Brandon Lacy Campos
Naked Poetry on YouTube
the retroactively ironic title, "I Live"
set against the previous in the playlist
unripe plums, metaphysics,
and Whalen's meditation
on William Carlos Williams

Looking up from the digital
to the IRL window
the derelict blue house
its gutters hanging down
the tree scorched by fire
the vacant lot diagonal
where the house so recently burned
under renovation to reclaim the poetry
of a previous century's architecture
gone in minutes of heat and electric fireworks
the lot now a graded smooth expanse
where once a firm frame structure stood
for a century or more

the sound of a car
tires crunching loose gravel

as it makes a U-turn
to head back up
N. Rampart toward Poland

The meditative insomnia of memory
keeps my eyes open lids heavy
scorched leaves hanging brittle and brown
empty lot now the city cleared it
only char marks on back fence remain
the repetition of traffic turning 180°
at the center of the intersection

This vacant lot is not the house
wood is not ash, nor fuel fire
this street a dead-end yet a means to one
imperfect impermanent interconnected

A small dog barks twice
walking by with its owner
      train whistle
        a carpenter's hammer

The living voice of dead poets
remembering dead poets
your words defy borders
the atoms of your body
expand out across the universes
in all directions and across all times

just as your legs spread wide across their limits
you defied their can'ts don'ts won'ts
and we love you for it

You live in ink in pixels in memory
your voice on the phone the week before
now more concept than cadence
the electric pop of dissolution
the unexpected news on Facebook
even before the cell phone rang

Sound waves can't be destroyed
the half life of your words' radiation
will never reach zero
I replay the video
permanently transfecting the cosmos
with the vector of your defiance
Brandon you are still fine as Hell

"Some moments..."

Some moments depression creeps in slowly
a subtle uneasiness in the gut.
A text message from an old acquaintance
bringing me to where I was.
Front and center with my aloneness.
The flutter of unease could so easily coalesce
as a microscopic blackhole
and with a metallic taste
I'd begin to be pulled into it.
A friend saying hey
from across the country
and I'd realize he too was not there.
He'd been there the last dinner
we'd had before the friend's relocation to Seattle.
He was at the restaurant ostensibly eating with us
but moving gregariously to other tables
alighting only for short moments.

Memory

Each memory is its own
discreet and distinct
Each a singular world
in an indiosyncratic solar system

An overflowing ashtray a stone cat
a glass of scotch a corncob pipe
The living face of a dead lover frozen in B&W
on an old fitness pass long ago expired
A dogearred paperback on Tilopa's song of mahamudra
Coming across a forgotten note in a half finished book
Hastily scribbled phone number on a napkin
in a pocket of jeans that no longer fit
Cigar wrappers in the pocket of your father's blazer
A pineapple doily where a candle melted
staining a rainbow into the cotton thread
The ghost smell of temple incense
remnants of agar and sandalwoods
The faint smell of perfume on a handkercheif
found in a discarded change purse
Underlining and marginal notes
in a handed down copy of *Leaves of Grass*
each fragments an accidental key

JASON CYCLE

The rocks will never miss you, nor the sky.
The sea will be unchanging, oh, my dear;
Tomorrow by the water, only I
Of all things else shall know you are not here.

—Ruth Moore

Prologue

I can still recall the first time I saw you
a grainy photo on the front page of the Daily Collegian
lips locked with my friend P.Z.
a kiss-in at the Student Union.
Shuffling through photos of a campus straight pride rally,
pink triangles warring with blue squares
on posterboard signs
Free Your Mind and your ass will follow,
I realize I had unknowingly captured you
rising above the countering crowd
like a figurehead at the prow of a ship
green military cap, Queer Nation t-shirt,
whistle clasped in your lips.

Running into you weeks later
at a five campus dance
tapping you as you walked by.
In between, Philipe had introduced us.
We chatted briefly and later heading
to last dance you found me again.
"You were supposed to be a one night stand,"
you admitted months later
hiding out through death threats
holding you after you learned
you had been outed to your parents
an anonymous envelope of newspaper clippings

feeling your tears again after you learned
it had been mailed by your best friend
your activist partner in crime
and two doors down on your floor
hearing of the tongue she was employing to curse you.

Sneaking into your dorm at night
listening to your roommate
breathing in the upper bunk
hours spent talking together
after he too came out
having the room to ourselves the next semester
your new roommate having moved out
after finding out you were gay.
Drinking taquila late into tomorrow morning
watching the blond ambition tour
snuggling and reading *28 Barbary Lane*
on a spring sunday afternoon.

No doubt it was fate that brought us together
and the same that edged us apart.
Hours and miles proved too much.
The insanity and insecurity of new boyfriends
tore impassable fissures between us
only fleeting stolen moments.
Banal conversation over thai
the last time I saw you.

One

Brunch at Fitzwilley's Tavern
the first morning after that first night
later parking at the Connecticut River
overlooking the retired railroad bridge
that is now the Norwottuck Trail

Orange leaves dropping silently
and the cradling smell of wet humus
the rail span to Elwell Island
Beginnings to Endings

Your uncompromising obsessions
guiding your life by
Madonna and 70s TV
Rhoda and Mary Hartman, Mary Hartman
your regular, rarely mitigated disappointments
recognition of the goodness in all people
perpetually undercut by their actions at the surface

We didn't separate for 48 hours
that first weekend
eventually torn apart
by the jealousy of friends
Years later, having lost touch,
I think of you while driving
through your hometown

That evening I pull up your facebook™ page
and see a concatenation of grief
how could you leave us
cant believe you're not here anymore
hope you found the peace you could not in life
I scroll back to your birthday
now ten months previous
two R.I.P.s a jarring contrast
to the sixty-eight Happy Birthdays

Your heart that would break
at the quiet innocence of an animal
yet allow no patience for yourself
dark clouds of pessimism and self-doubt
always hanging over you like a specter

Two

The intersection of history and possibility
we meet in the space between worlds
the small Siva lingam I bought you
sits at the center of a large svastika
ancient symbol of good fortune
emblazoned on a cloth draped
over a makeshift altar
the god garlanded in orange marigolds
the smooth stone surface glistens
from his recent bath in Ganges water

I cradle you as your body floats
in sacred water infused with oils
an armada of petals on its surface
You are in an improbable trance
held timeless in suspension
a realm between stark experiential reality
and the vast openness of the imagined

I lift you from the mother river
wrap you in white cotton
and bring you to your cushioned seat
I rub a layer of sacred ash
across your forehead
and hang a string of seeds
across your shoulders

and down your unmoving chest
I kiss your feet, my chela,
that you may be blessed
as your journey continues
till our next meeting
in shared dreams
of unexplored worlds
and shared memories
of the time before
the Blasted Tower derailed
your hero's quest
and suicide became
your mind's best option

Three

What does it matter
if you are dead
or simply dead to me?
The divide of minutes and miles
wedged between us by the crazy
that swirled around you
like a whirlpool
spiraling to emptiness

Four

quick dream kiss
while cleaning out
a patient's room
in an old age home
of the mind
quick to pull away
fear of being caught
by the bosses and spies
thrill of recognition
that we feel the same
surprised echoing smiles
waking to realize
it was you
half-sleep kiss
still warm on the lips
a somnambulant artifact

Five

I came across a picture of you,
underexposed and faded.
You're standing with Harry Hay
young fairy prince with his Saint.
This is how I remember you
the careful whip of your hair
the awe-inspiring smile
that dawned at the wonder
of an awe-inspiring universe
body glowing with combustible hope
before the inevitable moment of combustion
A time before anti-depressants and anxiety
warped your body and your world.
In a different time
and different place
you would have been
a great shaman.

Six

Our sacred topography is fading
AMC Harvard Square theatre
permanently closed
videos of your days as Rocky
in your gold lamé briefs
on Friday & Saturday nights
are degrading
to magnetic artifacts
Filenes 1881-2006 R.I.P.
Arsenic & Old Lace
Innovations In Leather
both gone too
I wonder if that place in
Cambridge is still there?
where you first
introduced me to Thai food
Date nights when
we were in the city

I hope you had
a coin for the boatman
and that you're now
enjoying exploring
the Last Museum.

Impermanence

I take refuge in the three jewels
the buddha, the sangha, the dharma
the awakened one, the community, the teachings
until I regain the clear sight of the Bodhimind
for the benefit of all beings

Metta

May the world be free of suffering*
the elderly woman spanging at the intersection
of Elysian Fields and N Claiborne
the hipster with his waxed mustache
tight black jeans and converse hightops
with his sign begging for art supplies
at the corner of Franklin Ave
the street rat on Decatur
who's too drunk to work
and too ugly to whore

may they be free of enmity
the 17yo who shot his friend
in the stomach on Canal St
6th shooting in 2 years @ Elk Pl
growing up with PTSD
a generation coming of age
in the overshadowed uncertain
decade post Katrina
loving grateful and kind

the surprised eyes of the 18yo
booked for rape statutory of otherwise
whose mother was too tired

to know where he was
on a Saturday night
healthy and at ease in all their ills

The smell of urine from a disused doorway
so strong you choke on its solidity
The scent of maid of orleans jasmine
dancing from a hidden courtyard
over a nine foot brick wall
topped with shards of broken glass
And find peace, embracing all conditions of life.

*Metta prayer adapted by Jundo Cohen for use at Treeleaf Zendo www.treeleaf.org

"the train whistle…"

The train whistle behind the house
resonant and throaty
I feel apart yet connected
to the circulatory system
of commodity and commerce
veins of iron flowing back
to the heartland
echoing the aorta of the Mississippi
as it flows toward the Gulf
the capillaries of the river delta
that took thousands of years to form
and man only 100 to destroy
the scars of industry
cutting unnaturally linear
lines through the cypress.

Dinosaurs in denouement

Evolution has passed us by—
unarrestable

We missed last call
at the mutation saloon

Just so many dinosaurs
waiting on the final stroke

ritualized buddhism
ritualized Xtianity

sitting silent
in the zendo

sitting silent in an alley
with 750mils of Mad Dog

Equally Buddha

The ground equally buddha
the dirt equally buddha
the rain equally buddha
the lone tree equally buddha
the brook, stream, river equally buddhas

the child equally buddha
the naked boy equally buddha
all women equally buddha
the poet, painter, vagrant equally buddhas

the trash of capitalism equally buddha
the repression of Leninism equally buddha
the falsity of Marxism equally buddha
the lie of democracy equally buddha

big business equally buddha
Coke, Burger King, MacDonald's equally buddha
trade, trust, tryst equally buddha
Islamic State equally buddhas.

Friendship

True friends are proof
of the universe unfolding
as it is meant to...

The subtle hand of the Architect
evidenced in old friends
appearing disguised as new...

Each day friendship
etches new inscriptions
on shared memory...

Echoing through the wood
in the reverberating crack
of a felled Christmas tree...

Carried across the morning
on the warming smell
of freshly brewed coffee...

"A clipping…"

A clipping from the local paper
photo of icicles and red berries
my father's handwriting at the edge
Thank you for this life!

Active alive
in the present tense
days before he died.

NOLA Zazen

The Zendo near our house in Maine
the sound of the han echoes off trees and hill
and large rock where Gato-Roshi's ashes lie.

The songs of birds chattering and trilling to each other
the mournful coo-ah coo of a pair of doves
and the cutting craw of a crow
the lone doe sidling her way silently
through the remnants of harvest
the resonant tonal croak of a bull frog in the pond
the strike of an early rising carpenter's hammer.

Here, the morning framed
by the warning of heavy equipment backing up
the rhythm of a train behind the house
broken by the sharp sound of poorly lubricated iron
wheels' screech on rail as it makes the turn
edging by the decommissioned naval station
the backhoe digging through gravel, shells, and river silt
repairing the gas lines beneath the street
the occasional siren from the fire substation
at the end of the next block
workers' voices raised over the noise of machines
five horns of a tug in the canal

and the answering clanging bell
as the drawbridge goes up
a car with bad muffler and loose belt waiting.

Behind the sound of rock on steal,
the sounds of two birds singing
a dog barks
another answers
a feral rooster crows WAKE UP

"A bucket…"

A bucket
of muddy water
becomes clear
after it sits

A disturbed
bowl of water
only settles
when still

The trees
are not affected
by the wripples
accross their reflection
when a frog jumps
in the water

3am Tweeker

Help Help me please!
The shadows… there
they are reaching out
of the shadows to grab me!
Naked wandering the next block
screaming into the night and alone
Stop torturing me!

The light through the bedroom window
and half-cracked door
reflects a luminescent barcode
on the opposite wall
thick columns of blue intercut
with a single blinking red bar
from the RR crossing light

The sound of breaking glass
Won't someone help me?
Anyone?! Please…
a solitary figure holding close
to the refuges of light
spilling beneath the street lamps

Root Guru

A single white cloud in a vast clear sky
condenses to rain and dissolves into the ocean.

A lamp ahead on the path that
teaches you to be your own light.

Borrowed VHS discourses
from the Nanda Meditation Center.

Fiery expression caught in analog
one eyebrow arched mischievously.

Finger raised look where it's pointing
eyes infinite see what they're seeing.

Light and sound travel at different speeds
a bolt and its thunder are not simultaneous.

Years of silence and seclusion pass
until despotic insanity pulls you back.

Videos on YouTube your Upanishad
interviews with the press your Last Testament.

Eyes glazed from pain or pills
hands slowed by years of nitrous.

The old fire still there below the surface
though dulled by a layer of addiction.

The wild geese over the water
do not intend to cast their reflections.

Silver Halide Crystals

Developer reduces the silver halide crystals
transforming light to precious metal.
Then stop bath, fixer, water wash.
A moment frozen in a magick mirror
of alchemy and chemistry.
The now becomes something made—
an object, an inverted window to minutes ago.

The shelter of the Claiborne Oaks
cut down to make way for I-10
now replaced by painted trees
on cement columns supporting the expressway
suffering the generation loss
of successive copying.
I look out over Tulane Avenue toward the river
Big Charity stands a toothless specter
the broken eyes of the tuberculosis hospital
red brick in the foreground.
A handsome man stands at the corner
of N. Robertson and Louisa texting
making the commute home worthwhile.

The smell of vinegar instantly
brings back memories of darkrooms.

Images rise to the surface in the developer tray.
Light became silver
transferred by light to silver again.
White paper transforms to ghostly icons
the burning building on Canal St
before the roof collapsed,
fire trucks and onlookers
the smell of wet char—
a drying rack of present moments
captured at 1/500 of a second.

Sorting through old negatives
an accidental shot captured on
an unnumbered first frame
underexposed silver phantom
of a sleeping friend
instantly invoking long hours delving
deep into richly loaded discussions
of magickal pagan kaos philosophies.
The irony of starting to read a Teutonic grimoire
the same day you say you're moving to Finland.
Connecting years later time has written
its difference on each of us
but also a powerful reminder
that deep friendship can abide.

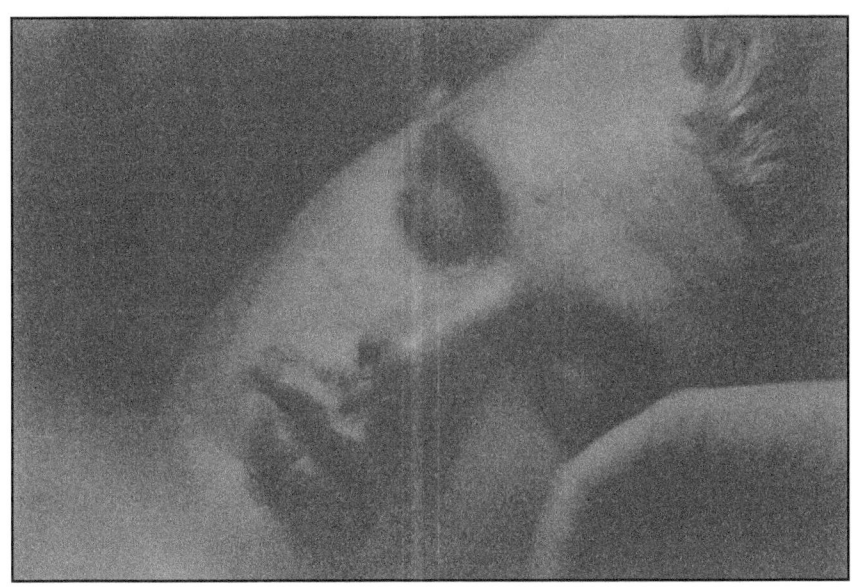

Sewing the Rakusu

A poem of bloody finger pricks
needle poking through green cotton
cho and *tan* grid of the front.
Reading Robert Aitken through Ango
preparing for the new year's *Jukai*,
precept taking ceremony.

In the midst of
tearing out threads
of misstepped stitches
the unexpected reappearance
of an old college friend
now turned dharma brother.
The *kechimyaku*, lineage chart,
an ahistorical bloodline going back
to the historical buddha,
a caligraphic bond between us.

The anchoring *joro* blocks
holding firm the inset silk reverse,
geneology of the Dharma,
red chop, and black calligraphy:
Ocean Literature
Kaibon-san, Just Sit!

The Impermanence of Never

The cruel sound of never
is it also impermanent?
You come and return.
Memories are ripples on the pond
echoing your present moments.

Is it my discernment that gives rise
to the harsh realness of never?
My distinction between you here
and you not here
and you gone from this world forever?

There is a time before we knew each other,
a time when we felt eternity,
and a time left to memories and momento mori.

There is a time when those who remember us
will return to the time when we never existed—
like dry leaves disintegrating to earth
in a forgotten graveyard swallowed by forest.

The Space Between

The contemplative stillness
that exists in that moment
between past and future;
the dimensionless point
between memory
and impermanence;
the intersection between
the world of humans
and the world of faery—
between hard flesh
and ethereal fay;
the interstitial space
of legend between
history and myth…

About the Photographs

Cover: Maine woods, 2012

Opposite page vi: Overflow XI – Jaume Plensa (detail), Sydney and Walda Besthoff Sculpture Garden, City Park, New Orleans, 2016

Opposite page 1: New Orleans, 2012

Page 6: Bywater Neighborhood, New Orleans, 2015

Page 11: Bywater, New Orleans, 2016

Page 12: Lafyette Cemetery No. 1, New Orleans, 2016

Page 17: Maine, 2011

Page 18: Salem Witch Trials Memorial, Salem, MA, 2008

Page 22: Ruth Moore, n.d., by Eleanor Mayo

Page 26: Moore-Mayo homestead, Bass Harbor, ME, 2017

Page 29: Moore-Mayo homestead, Bass Harbor, ME, 2017

Page 30: Marigny, Neighborhood New Orleans, 2014

Page 33: Marigny, New Orleans, 2016

Page 39: Sydney and Walda Besthoff Sculpture Garden, City Park, New Orleans, 2017

Page 44: Asticou Azalea Gardens, Northeast Harbor, Maine, 2011

Page 49: The "Rusty Rainbow" at Crescent Park, Bywater Neighborhood, New Orleans, 2014

Page 50: Mount Desert Island, Maine, 2011

Page 53: Oak Alley Plantation, Vacherie, LA, 2015

Page 63: Lakelawn Cemetery, Louisiana, 2015

Page 66: Jason McDonald and Harry Hay, date and photographer unknown

Page 70: Potter's field, New Orleans, 2011

Page 74: Buddha through a Hasselblad 500C/M, 2016

Page 77: Lower Ninth Ward, New Orleans, 2007

Page 78: Bywater Neighborhood, New Orleans, 2016

Page 80: Maine woods, 2014

Page 83: Maine woods, 2013

Page 84: Maine woods, 2012

Page 87: My father, 1989

Page 88: Morgan Bay Zendo, Surry, Maine, 2013

Page 91: French Market, New Orleans, 2016

Page 92: Garden District, New Orleans, 2016

Page 94: Graffiti, Bywater, New Orleans, 2015

Page 98: Vacant "Big Charity" Hospital, New Orleans, 2015

Page 101: Portland, Maine, 1994

Page 102: Maine coast, 2004

Page 105: Maine woods, 2014

Page 107: Enso by Enkhtuvshin on flickr (remixed, under creative commons license 2.0, https://creativecommons.org/licenses/by/2.0/) and "AH" by Allen Ginsberg, collection of the author

Acknowledgements

A special thank you and incomplete list of those family, friends, teachers, and poets who are echoed within the memories underlying these works or accompanying me on the photo walk abouts.

Maine: Norman Bamford, Evan Bryant, (ever my best man) Adam Carter, Jason Drost, Travis Erwin, Justin Koons, Billy Malay, Eric Olsen, and Lincoln Snowdeal

New Orleans: The Friendly Bar family

Steve Berman who has the dubious honor of being the first to suggest doing a collection of photography, Peter Dubé for hours of conversation

Erik Wahlstrom and Wallace Merritt for stoking the photographic fires.

For their guidance over the years: Jerome Leibling, Steven Bragg, and Jundo Cohen & the sanga at Trealeaf Zendo

First readers: Muriel Davisson, Chris DeVere, Shane Lucas, Jeff Mann, and Jennifer Munson

Inspiration: Allen Ginsberg, Antler, Gavin Dillard, Trebor Healey, Gary Snyder, and Emanuel Xavier

In memoriam:
Jason McDonald and Brandon Lacy Campos

INTERSTITIAL.GALLERY
THE SPACE BETWEEN

About the Author

Davisson has had a deeply rooted passion for photography since the first roll of Tri-X he shot with his parent's Miranda G SLR. He received a B.A. in photography and cultural studies from Hampshire College where he studied with Jerome Leibling and Carrie Mae Weems. A pioneer of rebel DIY publishing, Davisson produced the zine *mektoub* in the 90s and is currently the founding editor of *Ashé Journal* publisher at Rebel Satori Press. He is the author of the collections *The Starry Dynamo: The Machinery of the Night Remixed* and *The Star Set Matrix*. His story "Dim Star Descried" was selected for the 2009 edition of *Wilde Stories: The Best in Gay Speculative Fiction*. In addition his work has appeared in the anthologies *Suffering from the Night: Queering Bram Stoker's Dracula, Madder Love: Queer Men and the Precincts of Surrealism*, and *I Do/I Don't*, as well as the journals *Abrasax: The Journal of Magick and Decadence, Gnosis*, and *Ashé*. Davisson grew up on an Island off the Maine coast and now calls New Orleans home.